SKIRT FULL OF BLACK

SKIRT FULL OF BLACK
POEMS BY SUN YUNG SHIN

COFFEE HOUSE PRESS
MINNEAPOLIS, MINNESOTA

Coffee House Press books are available to the trade through our primary distribu-
tor, Consortium Book Sales & Distribution, cbsd.com or (800) 283-3572. For
personal orders, catalogs, or other information, write to info@coffeehousepress.org.
Coffee House Press is a nonprofit literary publishing house. Support from private
foundations, corporate giving programs, government programs, and generous indi-
viduals helps make the publication of our books possible. We gratefully acknowl-
edge their support in detail in the back of this book.

LIBRARY OF CONGRESS CIP DATA
Shin, Sun Yung.
  Skirt full of black : poems / by Sun Yung Shin.
      p. cm.
ISBN-13: 978-1-56689-199-8 (alk. paper)
ISBN-10: 1-56689-199-X (alk. paper)
  1. Adoptees--United States--Poetry. 2. Immigrants--United States--Poetry.
3. Koreans--United States--Poetry. 4. Korean Americans--Poetry. 1. Title.

PS3619.H575S55   2007
811'.6--DC22   CIP

2006038521

10   9   8   7   6   5   4   3
printed in the United States

This book is dedicated to the worldwide Korean diaspora—six to seven million overseas Koreans living in 140 countries.

CONTENTS

1

2

3

4

5

6

1

MACRO-ALTAIC

"Sometimes the surface forms defy etymology."

In place of reading, two doors open
away from each other. Door—paper—door—

One spine bends along a radius
of one. Finger bones like wingspan
of flightless bird. Travel
advisory to the following
nations:

Date on the red book from Korea, year prior to birth, folk tales, year of
gestation, folk tales, year of a maternal body with double interior.

Only during war does a house need two walls. A spare, a terminal—

White, the color of death, Western clothing.

*

"Korean contrasts structurally with European languages such as English in a
number of ways."

Your sister's spirit escapes through a pinprick in the paper wall.
The shaman kneels at her side as before a meal.

Eat the nail clippings of your sister; assume
her shape. Assume tiger, she–
bear, son of God.

Chew with your words closed.

*

". . . not easy to draw boundaries in any language between what is a word
and what is not a word and Korean is no exception."

In place of mother there was mother, both moving from crib to doorway, from doorway to departure, from doorway to arrival—

Paper, white, the color of a virgin, Eastern
clothing. Both mothers moving
from flame to table, four
legs and a back.

1987 symmetry at Chicago bank teller, bulletproof mouth, a machine translates money into *money*. Best rate of exchange:

Our palms break half-
open like fans, doors
on alien hinges—

*

"Over the years, the arguments for and against Chinese characters have been repeated, attacked, and defended countless times, often with great passion."

Go unspoken "Macro-Altaic." Go unwritten family name.
Go flower, flutter, flag.

*

"The issue has become largely academic." "It is difficult to hear the difference between *s* and *ss.*"

At the market, a moon–
shaped comb sorts hair still
bound by scalp. In the curtain
forms a white path.

KUAI-ZI

Animals think in pictures: Temple Grandin thought she was a cow:

Everyone in the audience began to twitch in their seats.

A woman whose son is autistic began to cry:

"He does not recognize me, his own mother!"

"We are cannibals," said a man to his wife, in a picture. He took a picture of the page of words and saved it for processing later.

*

THIS PERSON IS THE "STICKER," HIS JOB IS TO SLIT THE THROATS OF THE COWS AS THEY PASS BY ON THE ASSEMBLY LINE.

poem: movie: lamp: blast: shadow: reinvention

*

There is a false rumor that Confucius was a vegetarian and advised people not to use knives at the table because knives would remind them of the slaughterhouse.

"Can we please have chopsticks?"
"In Japan they're called *hashi.*"
"East Asian scholars who are from Iowa and Pittsburgh?"
"Ee-o-wah Peets-ber-goo-ruh"
"hashi?"

*

THIS IS THE "KNOCKER," ADMINISTERING THE STUN BOLT TO THE COW'S BRAIN.

coarse wood the color of late afternoon:
conjoined twins in paper envelope:
little brothers:

every pair one image:
porous organic matter absorbing flavor of meat or attendant seasoning.

*

Chinese chopsticks, called *kuai-zi* (quick little fellows with bamboo heads), are nine to ten inches long and rectangular with a blunt end.

*

IN THESE OPERATIONS, WHERE A MINUTE OF "DOWN TIME" CAN SPELL A LOSS OF MANY HUNDREDS OF DOLLARS.

"Everything in Asia is so old!"

At noon they have no shadows, but they are with their brothers—chronological peers for eternity. They should have no difficulty addressing each other with appropriate informality.

"The clay soldiers in their open tomb eat nothing but the light from the flashing cameras."

If they could speak, they might choose to communicate in images . . . being clay, they are porous and have passively absorbed the odor of death and the language of tourists.

"Each soldier is an individual."

OBVIOUSLY, THESE WERE HOME RATHER THAN OFFICE MACHINES, MEANT FOR PEOPLE OF LIMITED MEANS WHO NEEDED TO DO SOME OCCASIONAL TYPING

It looked rather like a sewing machine, because it was manufactured by the sewing machine department of the Remington arms company.

decorative
well-engineered
arms
repeating

By the 1920s, virtually all typewriters were "look-alikes"

only in capital letters: **QWERTY: WOMAN: TYPING: HARD RETURN**

woman: understroke or "blind" writer

we always wanted to swim for years without stopping
we can only see our hand in front of our face

This means that the typist (called a "typewriter" herself in the early days) has to lift up the carriage to see her work.

carriage: skirt: drawers: shades: ghost: confusion: lifting

The native carries goods to market to be bartered. She returns home with rice, salt, cloth. She strips to the waist at the river, singing work songs while beating clothing against wet rocks in the sun. Over time the basket shapes to the curve of her skull but we do not know if her head responds to pressure in the same manner.

Not everyone knows how to make paper from tree pulp: the paper is hit against the shuttle by a hammer, and then the paper collects in a basket.

You can take a class on almost anything these days.

woman: solid base of loyal customers
woman: well-engineered

... electrification, right up to the beginning of the word-processor era.
efforts to produce ... cheaper ... index ...

performs another motion ... print the letter ...

survive into the twentieth century (by typing)

FRUIT OF ARRIVAL

1

3:5 Then the herald cried aloud, To you it is commanded, peoples, nations, and languages,

The mare's second birth, a humble birth, persons of birth.

My mate cut the purple cord, I drop a kiss onto my son's birth, now closed and clean.

The navel a door closed like an ear, something smothered.

I never sang sweet lullaby, my voice has poor affect. The bones of my face, the back of my head, all flat as a cradle.

Aluminum, life. A mirror. An image. "One that closely or exactly resembles another; a double: *He is the image of his father.*"

Forefathers. God. "A mental picture of something not real or present."

2

3:5 that whenever you hear the sound of the horn, flute, zither, lyre, harp, pipe, and all kinds of music, you fall down and worship the golden image that Nebuchadnezzar the king has set up;

Most births, no herald, no golden image. No king.

Hospitals advise you to bring a photograph, or an image, of something that will help you give birth. Perhaps a picture of your first child. A flower.

Knit a necklace of clichés for this living grave, circle the boat, dip the oars into its dark silver taste.

This bird that glances off your shoulder. Name it and it will remain, repair its broken wing and it will bear monstrous fruit. Riches and golden robes.

3

3:6 and whoever doesn't fall down and worship shall the same hour be cast into the midst of a burning fiery furnace.

Women have called it the ring of fire. I did to myself call it a train from which I could not fall. Not a ring but a momentary house of fire, and from that white furnace a spark flew.

"Image: A reproduction of the form of a person or object, especially a sculptured likeness."

There was the long wet bite from the jaws of his scissors.

It takes years to hear with a closed ear, a stitched ear, disfigured.

Romance—a blood pressure cuff and a bloodshot eye.

4

3:7 Therefore at that time, when all the peoples heard the sound of the horn, flute, zither, lyre, harp, pipe, and all kinds of music, all the peoples, the nations, and the languages, fell down and worshiped the golden image that Nebuchadnezzar the king had set up."

A thick ribbon of disaster and the fairy-tale heads of wives roll ungratefully over the bedroom floor and down the stairs to the gut of the house.

"I just swept the stairs." We learn to rhyme wept, kept, leapt . . .

There may be asymmetry and it may be permanent.

The coat of nations slips too easily off some of our shoulders. The stink of desiccated fur, decoration. A king's collar. What for warmth.

A clean hit. Surgical precision. A nation divided. Distance mapped and commanded.

This head of state, a metal mind, a monstrous maternity.

Map our agitation, heartbeats and echo.

Death's milk-white mare and her sweet, sweet hay. A clean place.

IMMIGRANT SONG

All birds—even those that do not fly
—have wings

A constant confession
Admission of omission

This is your punctuated equilibrium
And everything in between
Slow it down

The moment of extinction
The death of the last individual of a species
(Let's put it aside for now)
Stay with it

This is our gene flow
How do you like our genetic drift
A riff, a rift, a raft . . .
Too rough for the second half

Take us under, take us downhill
Paint *pangenesis* all over your dancing body
The new party god
Keep the beat going, don't stop, you can't stop

Crick & Watson
Evo-devo
This is your mother's local phenomenon

If this is racial hygiene
Why do I feel so dirty?

Microcosmic soul
It's an involutionary wonderland
This living matter
A modern synthesis
4.6 billion years of biology
Can't stop the ideology
Graduate from meet/mate
To fitness landscape of sexual selection

From land over sea
It's a hard lyric
The impression of a key in a bar of soap
A transitional fossil

Keep camping
Plant the flag
Bury the burial mound
Put the *pop* in popular
And the *sigh* in science

2

ECONOMIC MIRACLES

Also this confusion about Korean names is further complicated by the fact that Korean women retain their maiden name even after marriage.

A visitor left me her calling card in a celadon bowl. Paper fish, a palm without fingers, an opaque windowpane to be pricked or burned with a cigarette. How high does a burning wall perfume the sky?

Is the visitor my enemy? Why am I teaching her English when she speaks almost as well as I? What a vast land: "almost." From Tokyo, she is half Korean & half Japanese and says to me in her breaking English, "We look so much alike we could almost be sisters!"

Lesson: poets are not qualified to teach Conversational English as a second, third, fourth, fifth language. My subversive thoughts were running away from our two-way mirror, out the room, under the door.

> Legally abandoned
> orphan
> foster child
> eligible for adoption
> immigrant
> legal resident alien
> naturalized citizen
> alien registration number A35300104
> passing for American-born
> passing for Chinese
> my maiden name even after marriage

*

I didn't know Jesus of Nazareth
had siblings. Aramaic is not even
my second language. And so my heart
leapt for Joseph. Our father,
who art in shadow.

The statues of Mary
show one swaddled infant, the first.

Held by her left
arm to protect her
heart or held by her right
arm to protect his?

*

*The family trees of most Koreans have been accurately kept for many centuries with
some traced to over 1,500 years. Koreans have pride in their ancestry and the origin
of their family name.*

One takes pride in a defect
such as poor eyesight. To have been born
in a time of spectacles is a miracle. Had I been
a nobleman's daughter, I would have been good
at ripping the seams out of clothing
to wash the pieces, but not good
at sewing them back
together. What sisters are for. What
mothers are for.

What servants are for.

At the eye doctor I fail to read my ancestral chart, the giant E combs the
giant white poster into a blurring rain. The chart reads me and while the
doctor turns away it wrinkles into a snicker. The black spoon's concave
palm momentarily protects the left eye from the scorn of the right. If eyes
could talk or mouths could read . . .

*

With their grace and poise the Korean women have much to offer
a modern society.

What has a modern society to offer us? Have the world's women formed a
government-in-
exile and where can I take the civil service test? How many poems shall I
write? How quickly shall I pass.

What shall we hide under our Western dress aside from our modesty? What
style modernity between millions of pairs of daikon legs?

*

24

Many foreigners coming to Korea hear about the Korean kisaeng and may even have an opportunity to attend a kisaeng party where they are royally entertained by a bevy of attractive girls. For the average Westerner this sudden flood of feminine attention is almost overwhelming. The expense of an evening with kisaeng recreation can leave a heavy dent in one's pocketbook, so be prepared.

I was not prepared
when the visitor took back her card
so quickly it nicked me across the cheek. And yet
I turned, and kept turning
the other one. I waited

for a matched set. I practiced
my English in my borrowed face and practiced
pretending to be half-Japanese.

My son says inside when he means outside.
He says close the door when he wants it opened.

*

The education of women was as impractical during the Yi Dynasty as sending the family cow to learn the Chinese classics.

A young girl could go far in the entertainment world if she showed real promise in creative poetry, which is the Korean sijo.

A poet learned in the art
of conversation! Counting syllables
for the *sijo*. Counting cups
of *soju* going down my host
father's throat. Though we may be cows,
we count, so be prepared for this sudden
flood of feminine attention.

*

The older kisaeng took great care in finding a ranking nobleman to spend the first night with the newly graduated girl. Throughout her entire life, the kisaeng was proud of her "first night man." The life of the kisaeng is short and they must retire at the age of thirty.

First night
first man
first life
first short
first retire
first age

Women at work. Poetry
not comfort. Classics
or cattle.

*

Scottish historian James Gale noted that "dancing-girls" and the laboring women were the only groups seen during the day . . . not often pretty in feature from the Western point of view, but striking . . . with never a shadow across her easy-sitting conscience; happy in the role she is called upon to play, and feeling that she is a very important part of what the East calls society . . .

Call upon our visitor with the celadon
bowl stolen from the museum for our first night
of poetry, of women's
work, of half-faced
miracles, of Western doors heavy
lidded as an Asian eye.

"Close your eye slowly, more slowly," the director of the documentary about war crimes against Koreans told me.

Slow like glass as a verb.

From open to close is a distance
of a few millimeters swept away
by a few sparse lashes, turned
down to protect the Mongoloid eye from sudden sandstorms.

Light reflects off my computer
monitor not the glittering
rice paddy, not the sewing
machine's glittering
needle dipping like a cormorant into tomorrow's
Nike and this is
the Culture at work.

From physiognomy to economy, what
does any sky know
of impracticality? What does woman know
of miracles?

FLOWER I, STAMEN AND POLLEN

"thread in the warp of a loom"
"a fine flour, dust"

                    *

*   *

The eleven brothers were princes, and each went to school with a star
on his breast, and a sword by his side. They wrote with diamond pencils
on gold slates, and learned their lessons so quickly and read so easily that
everyone would know they were princes. Their sister Eliza sat on a little
stool of plate glass, and had a book full of pictures, which had cost as much
as half a kingdom.

                    *

*   *

Telling the tale backwards forces me to begin with my mother's death—
timely, coincidental with my birth, which preceded or foreshadowed
or was a gross analepsis she could not have predicted. Chronotope.
A seared metal scar peels away and becomes my second mouth, stitched
tight. Perhaps she could have kept the drunk king out of the garden.
Perhaps the serpent and his pretty talk and his jeweled skin so changeling
in the summer sun. Perhaps when she wanted the fruit she would have
settled for the stem, the bark, the copper-flavored dirt licked clean off the
root, its many disappearing tendrils.

Going back to the beginning. Adorn the scene of the crime. Forgotten the
barbed body burned, the nest of smoke, the heart of ash, iron urn. Mouth
choked and sealed. Carbon stronghold. Natural to bear this pyre. Knit this
eternal coat, so coarse, a hide, my other skin, a furious work of nettle. Flax.
Sparrow-light. How I blister and bleed.

When the wicked queen saw this, she rubbed her face with walnut juice, so that she was quite brown; then she tangled her beautiful hair and smeared it with disgusting ointment, till it was quite impossible to recognize the beautiful Eliza. No one but the watchdog and the swallows knew her; and they were only poor animals, and could say nothing . . .

*

*   *

And a new-hewn enemy was fashioned from the beautiful Eliza, a girl with a walnut-juice face, nut-brown skin, and her glare a greasy blur. Nothing was impossible, she declared. Not even communion with the animals, dumb as she. Patron. Victor. Cloak of bitter tobacco leaf. "Speak zero, mark no one."

is God who makes the wild apples grow in the wood, to satisfy the hungry, and He now led her to one of these trees, which was so loaded with fruit, that the boughs bent beneath the weight . . .

        *

*   *

My life stood as a loaded (weight laden with warrant
My life stood as a wild (wood abundant with beasts and the nail trimmings of angels
My life stood as He (hunger *Aeiparthenos, Semper Virgo*
Satisfy me (beneath (tomb of meter and pitch
Boughs break (breath frost onto thy crown of twelve stars

to look once more at the palace where our father dwells, and where we were born, and at the church, where our mother lies buried . . .

*

*   *

Rules of the Storyteller:
1. Brother and sister shall seek repose in divided chambers.
2. Long before bearing vain weight.
3. Long before temple swords at side.
4. Shatter, little glass, shatter, thick with animal milk.
5. Turn trembling book, sown with images that we might know Her.
6. Dear kingdom, but half your cost.
7. Filament stalk and a nest of pollen.
8. And man was sprawling from dust and earth.
9. And his rib, his cage, his arbor of slinging hearts . . .
10. God-seed, obscure in birth and ruin.

But remember, that from the moment you commence your task until it is finished, even should it occupy years of your life, you must not speak. The first word you utter will pierce through the hearts of your brothers like a deadly dagger. Their lives hang upon your tongue . . .

        *

*   *

You must not speak. You must not. You must. You. The first word will
    pierce their hearts.
Your last word will pierce your own. Seven swords a flame on seven sorrows.
Son and brothers. A historical inheritance. If only your tongue were
    large enough
for all of them, the size of their lives. This task, this colossal silence.
Flesh, tissue, you gorge throbbing on the words.

By her side lay a branch full of beautiful ripe berries, and a bundle of sweet roots; the youngest of her brothers had gathered them for her, and placed them by her side . . .

*

*   *

Even the knot of her shadow reckoned him starlet, sparrow, hummingbird. Her youngest older brother. His devotion was positively medieval. Sanctified. Gilt. He had made a deaf rope of roots and her mute mouth stained abundant with the prophecy of berries. A replica of paradise. Their mother's womb he scraped clean. *Red-empty-red.* Her favorite lineage.

"If you are as good as you are beautiful, I will dress you in silk and velvet,
I will place a golden crown upon your head, and you shall dwell, and rule,
and make your home in my richest castle." And then he lifted
her on his horse. She wept . . .

           *

*   *

if (you tantalize me *Black am I and beautiful*

I (will translate genealogy my pearl my new luminous lexicon

dress (your inquiry black-stitched sheaf

I (will eyewitness Lamb of all seasons

golden circlet (your crown (dwell (decree exemplar out of fashion

if (you divine brethren diverge

beautiful (controversy nor the will of man

the archbishop shook his head, and whispered that the fair young maiden was only a witch who had blinded the king's eyes and bewitched his heart . . . All was not right with the queen . . . And now all the people came streaming forth from the gates of the city, to see the witch burnt . . . "See the witch, how she mutters! She has no hymn-book in her hand . . ."

                  *

*   *

Name her sacrifice for woman-girl.
Name her "keep thee" witch-girl. Name her sepulchre
Muttering queen. Revelations burn
Her invisible book, blank "formed the man of dust of the . . .
Pages. Name her Branch, grant (breath of life)
Her burning fresh (upon his face)
Fever. Her manuscript *I am black but comely*
Breaking her slender incarnation, a cloak
Back, its trembling compass.

Every piece of faggot in the pile had taken root, and threw out branches, and appeared a thick hedge, large and high, covered with roses; while above all bloomed a white and shining flower, that glittered like a star. This flower the king plucked . . .

          *

*   *

Not
Just any
Piece. Stamen traces a gambit
And pollen. Anatomy bursts the sutures
Sheltered with roses. So panoramic
Remote, this fine earth. Her
King, her pallid obscura, a pinhole
Blossom, her brothers
Stars and exemplars on their breasts and eleven
Diamond pencils to mark favor
Her name on their swan-wings, engrave accidents
Your marriage in illumination. Edge the ultimate. Immaculate
Shatter this deadly
(Mother who kneels before her son)
Sister, yield
(Announce)
Your shining
Flower.

3

THAT CAME TO BE SPLIT
INTO A PLURALITY

That we each have a number assigned to us
Thanks be to the devil for the idea of sequence

That we each have forgotten our numbers
Thanks be to the gods for a child's memory

That we each have a name, or three, assigned to us
Thanks be to the devil for sound marrying sense

That we each have forgotten the way to our house, apartment, farm
Thanks be to angels for the scent of chrysanthemums

That we each were the consequence of war, poverty, illness, death, despair, or hope
Thanks be to each other for what we call *society*

That we each will be buried with the bodies of our mothers
Thanks be to the stars for the constancy of matter that cannot be destroyed

That we each will be buried with the bodies of our fathers
Thanks be to the metal that will unskin the world

THE HOUSE

It was to be a permanent set, with permanent players
A serial

Take my hand and look, look at the costumes
pretending to be real clothes

No one had told them

Now here is a wool coat with no shoulders
Pinholes of army green

Punctuation with no words

A silk tie but no neck

An oven but no roast

Tea waits forever in its canister to release its perfume

Here is the roll of tickets
Pretending to be useful money

Here is the fruit from this, its own country
Its flesh still stippled as if painted

Here are the flies jewelling the windowsill
Imitating the necklace and earrings nestled in a box inlaid with mother-of-pearl

And look, child, here on the dining room table,
Can you just see?
Plates still around, like blind mirrors, like four open mouths—o

MYOPIA

"Cover your right eye"
"In my teens I experienced a bout of kleptomania."

"Can you read the first line?"
"I was arrested, fingerprinted, and released with a record to be expunged
  when I turned eighteen."

"How long ago did you start wearing glasses?"
"I survived my one hundred days. I survived to twenty-eight."

"Any other problems today?"
"I hide, hoard my food."

   •

"Are you Chinese?"
"Like most Asians, I have terrible eyesight."

"I'm Filipino."
"Like ripe fruit I watch my daughter's eyes to see when they will go bad."

"I'll give your records to Tammy up front."
"I haven't used a typewriter in years."

"You have a good day now."
"I can see the house in which I was born, but I can't

see my hands. I don't see what they've done until it's too late."

ONE RADIO

One woman hides her food under pillow, hoarding as a once-beaten dog hoards (though the bowl brims with) fresh meat.

Another releases invisible ovum after lost ovum into white napkin: envelopes *For Rorschach, For Freud, For Father—Ha Ha Ha.*

Butterflies with the face of her psychotherapist paper her dreams with their blood-russet wind.

*

The last grows child after child, a magical washing machine.

Accumulate, immaculate alchemy. In old Hmong way: thirty days of chicken & rice. Old every way: leaking breasts & previous children repeat themselves like rain.

discouraged : disuse

I ate lychee once and nearly clawed my gums to tears. Milk turns to cramps and I know my childhood is finished.

*

A queer horse is clothed in butcher paper, and so is the woman. The stirrups wear soft blue socks. *Dilation and Curettage* sounds old-fashioned, for an old-fashioned problem. The metal bed of instruments rests atop a papered bed.

(Little Boy Blue come blow your horn for the animals have all gone quietly, leaving sweet hoofprints in the snow.)

*

The word *spontaneous* now recalls a shower drain with many round mouths. Listen. Frequency. A pitch too high for humans. For one human. o, o, o.

"We have an oral tradition captured on paper." Miss Anonymity, my ear horn tucked under my robe, fiddling with the dials. Locate this pitch. This is how we find each other.

A KOREAN SUBTRACTION

Take out the dog's boiled skeleton but leave in the whinnying shudder.

The soup but the pot's evil empty gleam.

The blade but the knife's tainted handle.

The ring, dial, & cradle but the recognizable tone of voice.

The corpse but the coffin so we have cradles for the orphans.

The parents but the children and their crowns for the king who is cousin to his queen.

The rape but the ring of fire, the child, the evidence in triplicate.

The words but the poem: lungs & larynx, hard palate & tongue, alveolar ridge & lips,

aspiration, final stop.

The swiftness of the hooded shape, the child(hood).

THE TRUE STORY OF REFRIGERATOR AND MEDICINE CABINET

THE BOAT filled with parallelograms of milk

yolks waiting to break | into light

a rectangle incandesces | a half

     mirror, razor, hand basin

                 guests of the rectangles swept away white
evidence

EVEN THE ANIMALS DRINK Narcissus | draw themselves on the sides
of the dwelling|

inscribe us | chalk on the ramparts of the earth

       milk, clotting | blood, invisible | ink

THREE SQUARES A DAY and what have you got to show for themselves

wooden boxes, ice
     delivery | milk (man)

          your first | tablet swallowed

mortar or pestle

     now artificial amber   proof (of) child

         doors | apprehending

               their own (hinges)
magnetic (b)ride further

SAIL WAYFARER through kitchen, loo, century
         a body never wash(es) | in the same river twice

MISSING MASKS: NAMES

Kyop'o = Overseas Korean

Omoni = Mother

Aboji = Father

≠

Daughter (Ttal) with Many Sons

Son With Many Titles

Daughter Who Eats Whiteness Whole

≠

Practicing Catholic

Grateful Citizen

Lucky Emigrant

≠

Desire (Fever)

Hunger (Wayward)

Surrender (Arrival)

≠

A woman painted in yellow wax and doused in feathers, chrysanthemums, and all manner of earthly customs shall return for official measurements. She shall attempt to record the undeniable surfaces of the world. Failure is not a deterrent.

KYOP'O (OVERSEAS KOREAN)
ON LOCATION

Hanguk ► Korean ► English ►

Konglish ► Kinglish ► Queenglish ►

inglish ► inklish ► ink (this)

►

[silence in | of translation] [transcription of | in infancy]

►

All this because, after all, the train wreck speaks for itself, does it not?

When the time comes—as the parents have once spoken for the child—so shall the child speak for them.

"Sign here, please."

►

tongue : petals
bed : grave mound

the nature of the social order
official system

noumenon *(ri/li)*
phenomenon *(sa)*

►

"Thus, scattered references to the subject not only are fragmentary

"They have many superstitions and taboos: in the event of illness or death, they always abandon their old dwelling, rebuild, and resettle

HALF THE BUSINESS

Even now the devastation is begun,
And half the business of destruction done.

—*Oliver Goldsmith, "The Deserted Village"*

1

The word *hospice* first meant a shelter or lodging for travelers, pilgrims,
    foundlings, or the destitute.

2

She lay down, but not herself, onto the nursery bed.
God, give us the wit to let our wit outrun us.
A face inscribed with neglect, so her makeshift life began to mineral.

3

We should all have two languages, one of our childhood, and one
    of our deathbed.
God, let these two be the same.
No more songs about bureaucrats, armies, a confetti of human hair.

4

The pianist made a laying of hands as if to heal, or hear.
God, let these two be the same.
This sober vision, stitch it with needles made of peacock feathers and
    cherry stems.

5

A common marital miseducation. A sharp schooling.
God, let our narcotic grief outlive us.
May the words run swiftly across the palms of presidents, palm readers,
    a smoke trail in the sky.

6

She ceased to write even her own name, or handle her own money, or see
    anything but light and silhouette.
God, let the word *nurse* come to mean action.
Three women in a house speaking three languages. An unforeseen arrangement.

7

She had a name, like her silver hairbrush & mirror, now ill fit to use.

God, show us all the animals inferior to man so that they may name us
according to their wants.

Catalog these sounds so we may savor the fruit of inferiority.

8

Technology would choke on posthumous concerts but that it lacks
a singular throat.

God, lend your undergods, your minor children, your elapsed and nameless.

A mutual neglect, a wedding ring on the buried finger.

9

Every woman a scholar dissecting her own body, eating her own words
until the end of words.

Dear God, give no more speech or speeches.

This is the business of language, its livelihood. Even now. Even to begin.

4

FLOWER II, CALYX

"to conceal"

              *
*   *

blazing corolla (sweet apparition
bud of smoke (ruptured confession
kaluptein (permanent
shroud of paradox (embrace an import of ivory
this maiden portrait (graveside signature
maternity (prototype

*

first there was a sword (glint of heavy elements
made to pierce (tender
my only-heart (cherry wounds
drunken fruit (as lightning falls from heaven

*

*   *

take the temperature of my shade (election of the four-lettered lord
lacquered mask (skirt forbidden borders
of blush (under this
dark bell (embroidered iron signs
stain (stay
a spell (shoreline sewn with borrowed artifacts

*

then the word (made
flesh (among us

*

*   *

breathe nectar-script underwater (sightless
eat priestly (mute inheritance
consume husk & shell (sanctified conduit my bridesmaid's marrow
burn (milk (be downstream from thy countenance
plural (the horse and his rider

*

innocence (dye me *showy*
woman (surface palms

      *
*   *

shield this deep (indivisible aroma
green (assembly
of sepals (stem this throbbing chlorophyll throat

*

calyx (our
sex (I am still
waiting whitely
to spread (to fathom his retina (his coast borrows color

THE STATE WILL BE SERVED EVEN
BY MY HAND ON THESE LETTERS

Through the smoke
I remember that, in English, flammable
& inflammable are identical.

Serve up the dust pollinating foreign dust until you cannot distinguish
language of clay using delicate bones
of the inner ear. That hidden ivory snail is a slow learner!

My white feminism leaking as milk from the corner of my child's sleeping
mouth?

Light of this century, A.D. the thread of Christ, a line of poetry
marching left right, my children will never know
miracle of typewriter, perhaps even nostalgic
plans for obsolescence.

On television we are served a moveable feast of ticker tape news—
a dream in reverse, a relief or horror that the letters move
right to left . . .

and in this manner
we in borrowed language read on the page
downward—

the extinct chink & ting of machine
expertly kerned text makes swimmer's
turn at edge of page, spilling off
lower perimeter into excess
of darkness, the letters jockey for position but tangle in broken limbs
stray musical notations are crushed for their outrageous deviance.

in service to one composer
this is the public domain
these are the free sounds, available for reproduction

Shake out the page into the fragrant atmosphere above your lap
letters as dying flies, your skirt full of black
wings & legs still grinding, spinning.

OVER THE COURSE OF SEVERAL DECADES FOLLOWING THE KOREAN WAR, SOUTH KOREA BECAME THE WORLD'S LARGEST SUPPLIER OF CHILDREN TO DEVELOPED COUNTRIES

Some(where a) woman wears

the face once given. Possessions

scarce we go halves on slant

of eye & span of palm with cousin & other

ghosts. Where is the man with the face lent

mother? Fathers rare; *infant found*

at Shinkyo police station box—official

shoes careened around fortune of *Name*

& birth, pin &

note. Elsewhere (Norway, Australia)

another Korean

National bears the imprint

of my din. Cribs, nurse, hands, rice-milk powder, down

& rocked—carefully dated

checks. American/Father

asks *Why.* We don't speak. Years

burn to decades, this permanent

occupation.

TIN BULLETS : TINY BULLS : BULLETINS

At the Chinese restaurant in the strip mall my cheap jasmine tea enters one
end—blood weeps out the other. Two bags in the teapot huddle for strength.

Two pillows gossiping about their past lives
before cut and dried. A sigh
rises from the barrel of the pot.

Napkins, please, for the sister-
mouths who speak

in broth. Here flying fish may breathe:
choke: hallucinate

*

A religious white hat: medicinal: flag: sail: horizon: fortune

*

Just in time sold to English.
*Any later and I would have had to do it myself, but would not have known what
price to demand.*
My tiny scales, one grain at a time.

sold to amnesia.

sold for
        a face with a permanent rain of freckles, common as cement—
        foreign meat & milk—
a sister cold inside me, still five years old, a blue & white uniform
brushing her hidden knees—
a virgin bride, my dress soaking up everything it touches. Even filth will
turn to cloth—

*

train: veil: cloud:
blanket: evening: leaf

from a giant tree: god's palm: trans-
parent: fear

*

Message in a fist: lucky numbers in a chamber. Pry my fingers one by one . . .

You are a horse being broken for the first time by a gentle master: an iron
bit for the first time. Iron in your mouth, iron under your hooves . . .

The cow in the field seems idle as you trot away carrying him on your
leather-bound back: her skin on your skin under his skin.

*

tail: flag: a lady's brush (painting or hair)
your black eyes: shades

mise en scène & quick cuts

Pull down, pull down, your stall bears your scent: the rich air closing around
a missing shape—horse: girl

SPEED

As ever and always, there were

a series of possible solutions
broadly accepted international instruments
current practices are often in violation of these norms

Of the momentum of miniature automobiles racing under the furniture

Of the tempo of your canine's age, dry outline of his heat

Of the velocity of your child's life, not as a kite's white twine unspooling above
the green earth. Heat from friction against your palm, counterclockwise.

———————————

As ever and always, specifically in the

aftermath of the Second World War
ad hoc humanitarian response
all countries where emergency situations prevailed

Weight of childhood, the one red of his shirt worn for six months
    until outgrown

Size of the body, does the soul grow to meet it

Burden of the soul, can the body ever contain it

Only our breath is porous, only our lungs taste this air of yours

Identical words waiting beneath your teeth

One's tongue a singular burden

———————————

But newly, something new, something a degree different from what happened before,
but no more important than what happened before (or what shall become of this)

new generation of abandoned or orphaned
many of these children were Amerasians, fathered and left behind
   by U.S. servicemen
as did their Vietnamese counterparts a decade or so later

Human skull reaches adult size by age eight

What we once called vocal chords we now call folds

Science, like Adam, names and then—upon new intelligence—renames

Learn quickly that all cries are not musical

————————

Everyone. Each one of us. No one of us.

sharing responsibility for the burden facing the newly decolonized nations
domestic/intercountry/international
"mass exportation"

Closet full of your father's suits, his color-blind eyes, his asking, is this blue
or brown? green or maroon?

What we call vocal quality is subjective, what we call color

Garden, the yellow tulip bulbs unplanted, those withered skulls

Trivia of one's house, one's borders

Disfigure them freely, implant, transplant

Wash the lintels with blood

————————

It's always this kind of language that makes its appearance

a full-fledged and clear "demand"
for adopted children has continued to rise in the industrialized
    world, fertility has fallen
"structural supply of children"

Through this we shall pass, though not unmarked, though not without
marking this very air with our swiftness

Phenomenology: the word my friend and I always forget: "A philosophy or
method of inquiry based on the premise that reality consists of objects and
events as they are perceived or understood in human consciousness and
not of anything independent of human consciousness."

Or, the study of relations between the knower, the known, and knowing.

_____

*This Western sense of time. Fanciful verb tenses. We are tense with the time in our
words. On our hands. Idle. An innocent phoneme, one after another, like boots,
unknowing, attached to the knower*

today as in the past the United States is the world's foremost receiving
country of foreign adoptive children, responsible for roughly half of all
adoptions

often moratoriums are called to allow for investigation of abuses

We embrace her, Mother.

Selflessly, she. Taste of negative space around her robe.

Visitation, astonishing speed.

The long wake of the birth, wide bridal train going forward in time,
floating over the world, full of Christ-bearers.

Hands occupying the skin over hearts, hands shaped like a flag, skies light
with witness of clouds and bombs

GOD'S GRAMMAR TEST

God speaks in complete sentences, as He
Invents

As though a typewriter made of tissue and joint

God speaks in the present tense, as He
Believes in presence

Some languages are as circular as the whorl of a snail's shell

God writes with the smallest bodies, as they
Disappear back into era, moment, tracing a corridor

Fingernails made smooth by sand

A list with no dimensions
No demons
Written in throat-colored ink

We are terrified of His technology
(Genius)

We are mortified by His capitalization
(Permanent)

He addresses an audience
Rigid with rot

The breast of a soldier:
Photograph, a letter of letters

A sharp pin fixed to a methodical face
A bit of bright ribbon or perhaps stylized wings

5

VESTIBULARY

INTRODUCTION

The Korean language has a large number of speakers—almost seventy
million, more than the population of England or France, making it the
twelfth largest language in the world.

Hangul, the Korean writing system, was commissioned by King Sejong in
1443. Five of the seventeen consonants were created as the basic letters and
their shapes were based on the organs of articulation (lips, tongue, teeth,
palate, throat . . .) Furthermore, three of the basic vowel symbols were
"constructed to symbolize the natural pattern of the three great powers
of the Neo-Confucian universe: Heaven, Earth, and Man."

Contrary to popular Western conception, the Korean language is distinct
from Chinese and has genetic affinities to Altaic or Japanese depending on
the linguist asked. Government documents and professional writings continued
to be written in Chinese until the end of the nineteenth century, but with
the existence of *hangul,* the common people had access to a writing system
that was wholly Korean. "By calling it 'the Correct Sounds for the
Instruction of the People,' Sejong showed that he had created the new
writing system with the intent of bringing literacy to the ordinary citizens
of his kingdom, the 'common people' who were not of the intellectual elite
proficient in Literary Chinese." [1] Until the 1900s, it was called "women's
writing," which indicated its lower status compared to the terribly difficult
hanja. Today it's the people's language and Korea has one of the highest
literacy rates in the world.

I used the *hangul* characters and (the old Romanization)—their orthography,
form—to create bits of narrative and images inspired by their shapes.
The eros of language acquisition. We are the hunted and the hunter,
submitting to the demand of the utterance.

[1] Lee, Iksop and S. Robert Ramsey. *The Korean Language.* New York: SUNY Press, 2000.

	ㅏ	ㅑ	ㅓ	ㅕ	ㅗ	ㅛ	ㅜ	ㅠ	ㅡ	ㅣ
vowels ► consonants ▼	(a)	(ya)	(ŏ)	(yŏ)	(o)	(yo)	(u)	(yu)	(ŭ)	(i)
ㄱ (k,g)	가	갸	거	겨	고	교	구	규	그	기
ㄴ (n)	나	냐	너	녀	노	뇨	누	뉴	느	니
ㄷ (t,d)	다	댜	더	뎌	도	됴	두	듀	드	디
ㄹ (r,l)	라	랴	러	려	로	료	루	류	르	리
ㅁ (m)	마	먀	머	며	모	묘	무	뮤	므	미
ㅂ (p,b)	바	뱌	버	벼	보	뵤	부	뷰	브	비
ㅅ (s,sh)	사	샤	서	셔	소	쇼	수	슈	스	시
ㅇ	아	야	어	여	오	요	우	유	으	이
ㅈ (ch,j)	자	쟈	저	져	조	죠	주	쥬	즈	지
ㅊ (ch´)	차	챠	처	쳐	초	쵸	추	츄	츠	치
ㅋ (k´)	카	캬	커	켜	코	쿄	쿠	큐	크	키
ㅌ (t´)	타	탸	터	텨	토	툐	투	튜	트	티
ㅍ (p´)	파	퍄	퍼	펴	포	표	푸	퓨	프	피
ㅎ (h)	하	햐	허	혀	호	효	후	휴	흐	히

kiyek ㄱ

stained raw your lover's knee,

precipice;

scythe, raw grain;

late, wet harvest;

half-chair in silhouette.

niun ∟

Visual signals are sent to the brain about the body's position
in relation to its surroundings. Foreign fragments sewn. Shroud.

A borrowed shovel bit the soil while I beaded a prayer on bended
knee. Outside, a blackbird took a view of the church's corner.
Autumn brings the wet kiss of a deep red leaf.

tikut ⊏

arched tongue against hard palate;

hard arms of a handmade chair, open;

proscenium arch, invisible

maxilla & mandible ravenous with klieg lights.

liul 己

Dictionary of myth. A child in her library. Sounds eaten whole.
A bull and a virgin.

The lonely Minotaur haunted in broad-backed, forbidden heat.
His human clothes remained in two suffocating wardrobes, pinna
to pinna. On all fours he tried a wrecked ladder, a hoof slipped while
he had a vision of a snake meandering the legs of a four-poster bed.

mium ⬜

white room—green field—silk square;

single tooth, lonely tongue;

vacant cradle, empty pillow;

palm print on brushed steel.

piup ⊟

Bring a list of symptoms to your doctor.
A broken rope. Story.

A man stares out the window in drunken gravity, holding a glass half
full of sheer whiskey. His wife lays down among the fur coats,
unknowing of her womb half full of heritance. She palms a book,
open, margin mislaid.

sios 人

legs wide, skirt night–edged;

legs unlocked to Lower Kingdom;

fingers fine promenade, a feast.

iung ○

The soft palate rises to close off the nasal cavity. Sometimes a stent.
Or missing. Intervention.

She reads in a guide book about the chrysanthemum seeds & foreign
pollen and thinks of the barely male bees the queen rejects.
A flower turns to the sun spot, black retinal fire.

ciue 不

hanging, an execution of duty;

crow approaching unfamiliar limb;

letter folded into flag;

infinite tympanum of God.

chiuch 夭

"Historical accuracy"

A woman does an unseemly grave-dance, a bareheaded courtesan,
her flash of white neck through the cemetery gates.
She remembers a schoolgirl on seesaw, midair, her betrothed,
grounded. "Brings [history] alive."

khiukh ㅋ

backwards feather, floating on water;

soft palate closing your throat (guard at palace gate);

atomic weight of flight;

two fingers beckoning dusk.

thiuth 巨

Practice makes a lineage of disfigurement. Retrain the articulators.
Stubborn.

The girl pulls the ivory comb through fresh, oily wool while her
mother grips a broken broom, "Daydreaming daughter."
Tomorrow's phoenix claw may lay first fire-branches to burn three
swollen rivers & a choking dam.

phiuph

taiko drum & its faithless woman;

house & its vain, promiscuous entry;

my unbolted window, falling

fruit, ruinous bruise.

hiuh ㅎ

Vocal folds open. A passage of air through the pharynx.
Puff of white.

The sound of heat, her, heart. A sparrow hops over a leaf
on a boulder. We are busy bowing to brides & broken headstones.

a ⊢

A man with solitary arm, ghost

war, phantom companion;

next year's wife, her double

embrace.

ya ├

A syllabary of stones in the mouth. A museum of noise.
Broken knowledge.

We can only imagine bestiary's horn & spring rut, but the switch
from crab apple tree is real, as resin on cheap violin bow, the shape
and silence of your cursed wooden infant.

[schwa]　ㄱ

jade bud, slant branch;

radial seam of dragonfly;

ragged nail across lover's back,

incarnadined, ruby.

ye ㅋ

Due to the subjective nature of language, pronunciation will vary
from person to person, region to region.

A fist made bloody love to vodka-shined mirror while outside
a nation's banner at half-mast. He kissed the missing pieces,
struggled to love his knuckles.

o   ⊥

gold necklace, unhooked, touching my palm;

endurance of unfurled fiddlehead fern;

first crack across your wedding plate.

yo ⅃⅃

the master never was kind to that horse.

The room was left in violence, a disarray, the bed upturned, the woman upturned. The bedhangings mingling wantonly with the gossip forgotten on the lead paint of the windowsill.

u T

unfasten

to surrender

no hands for fair flag, no cotton cloth nor silk shirts;

yield

your uniform of wind & twilight.

yu ㅠ

Read left to right, just like in English. Practice. Even messily.

All fours & evolution. For salvation wash fresh blood over
the lintel. For a boy, nail red peppers above doorway.
Confuse yourself and remember this Vietnamese proverb:
Peppers are hot, all women are jealous.

ironed cloth on virgin's lap;

unfinished bow, stalled hunter;

master's pencil, waiting for you to sharpen;

body alone on cot, parallel;

body named death, eternal.

i]

This artifact. Anacoluthon. Distant country.

A woman unspooled a length of copper filament. Later that night she experimented on a spine. She had a taste for it. An addiction to salt and the resonant cavities of the human skull.

6

LEFTOVERS

"I'm a Gay Dad"
ᴛ-shirt on a young Korean man
Holding hands lightly with his girlfriend

"Pity, all of this Westernization"

The English language is true
Nonsense, everywhere

Make formal what was shaped by an individual hand
Paint it on cloth like a flag
A country of slogans in a foreign language

There will be schools enough

It was only hence
(those edible icons: chocolate bars and chewing gum)
A green Jeep in slow motion
And black children with an Oriental eye

The word *w-a-r* is too brief
For such a long bedtime story

Now I lay me down to sleep
To have a third hand to do the laying
To put the plant in its place in the garden of many

Hothouse logic

This cutting isn't making it
Too young, too old, too sick, too wet, too dry, too sad, too happy

Everything outlives us
The camps keep following us

Even our fingernails defy death
No longer digging, scratching in the dirt
Ten tiny spades
Pressed down by the harvest hand

THE VANISHING TWIN

One day we woke and our mother was a nurse
One day we woke and our father was a soldier
One day, with a blind hand, we searched the bed beside us, and suddenly
We missed our vanishing twin

Oh but remember our first bed!
That dark, red, humid place
The din
Our gills and webbed feet
Churning the master chamber
We were dazzling lazy fish

S/he was beautiful
Like us
We were one, we were three
We had no need for numbers
We invented zero

And when we split the atom
Sane went insane
Bravery to cowardice
Peace to war
God to godless
Parable to parade

Then you lost everything, shrank to a point smaller than this period .
Signaling the end of a breath

The syntax of human lungs and tongue

The work fell to me
To be a woman, or a man
To live and embrace its finish
To leave the aftertaste for others

Twin, other face
Dear one
To sign your name
To hold your signature
I see in the distance
A sleeping child under a man's umbrella

I cannot see his face

Only the miniature canopy
And its curtain of water

It's a bird, your signature
A crow, a raven, its oiled feathers

This umbrella
Protect me

Its lean wings, bones, and spine
How I love you
Your fine black flourish

NATURAL VARIATION

Most animals are satisfied with their gifts, their deficiencies
There is always one

Most animals are satisfied to mate with their kind
To rise and reduce, sand dunes and swamps

Some approach Buddha, some pass a hoof in the dirt before Adam
Some want names, others a yoke,
A bit, a ring through the nose, all their children dismembered, taken to tables
God knows where

When we lived among them

There are twelve, and in their black meat they hold our fortune
We serve it to our children
And season after season, they gorge
Throwing back their perfect heads and laughing
At the animal bending knee to the gods
Wanting more until he is proven a fool
Nursing the beauty of his wounded desires
Providence

A promise the length of a knife, the width of an oven

Go home, they sing
Wearing animal-head masks
Rocking on the four legs of their chairs
The scent of God all over them
Obedience, a pattern
Smeared across their lips

WORSHIP

Shall not we say that
We will sing for our supper

There is a prime number
That begs to be reduced

Resist the beggars
They have no rights

Is this Mass the same everywhere there is God
Even though different people eat differently

Teeming ancient cities
Hidden away in the jungle
Untouched by modernity
Until
Will they
No one can say

When logic feels cold to the touch
And tastes like metal
And won't digest
And won't pass through
The crucifix will turn to flesh, the man to wood

I got off the train at just the right time
To avoid my own destruction
But my feet ache in the rain

If we were to be fit together again
Like lost brother and sister
I could destroy the ice queen
And the palm of my foot would lose the shape of your cheek
And become again a place to meet the earth

You see I have stepped on you so often you have gotten used to it
And I am invisible

If I can't help you
I won't look at you

You won't have to endure it ever again

I read about us in books in order to understand
How we can be so unimportant
Twenty-six letters make a linear home
A margin of barbed wire fence
Around our pen, our paragraph

Here's what always happens

I'll count, you recite
I'll hold the pages, you turn

Long division
A long look in the ice cold
Blink, a wrapper of lashes

UNTIL THE TWENTY-SECOND CENTURY

I laid my childhood to rest at the end of the tracks of the twentieth century
Like Hansel's breadcrumbs
And they were eaten by birds and small, wild animals
A deer caressed his three-pronged antler against the mossy bark at the edge
    of the forest
He was too great for crumbs
He was too slow to notice

God knows I have rarely been in a forest without fear
It knows when to combust, turn seeds to bombs

I laid my motherhood along the beginning of the skyline of the twenty-first
    century
Like Hansel's pebbles
They will balance on the sky's uneven floor
Until I retrace and pick them up, lining my pockets
Or they, as rocks have done, are mistaken for food

Since we have robots and monsters
To clean, grind, entertain

God knows I am rarely near a true rock without fear
How it notes the era by shedding its skin
Every time it meets rain, wind, a rough tumble

Who knows old age is coming

Or shall be skipped over the space sewn by a bird
Who lights upon a second branch

If you wait for me, I will meet you in the twenty-second century
After the crumbs and pebbles are spent and lost in this one

If you wait for me, I will consign my bones to a place
That is neither trail nor time

Make an ivory needle from my ring finger

Wait, and I will make a map in this leaf-darkness
Not trace or terror

I will make for you a master key
Until then, I will wear it smooth

CREDITS

Grateful acknowledgment is made to the editors of journals where these poems first appeared, sometimes in different forms or with different titles:

Ache Magazine: "Myopia"
Barrow Street: "Obviously, These Were Home Rather Than Office Machines"
Court Green: "Half the Business"
Indiana Review: "Macro-Altaic"
Mid-American Review: "Economic Miracles"
Swerve: "Flower I, Stamen and Pollen"
Water-Stone: "Over the Course of Several Decades Following the Korean War, South Korea Became the World's Largest Supplier of Children to Developed Countries"
WinteRed Press: "Vestibulary"
Xcp: cross cultural poetics: "Kuai-Zi"

WORKS CITED

Adams, Edward B. *Korea Guide.* Korea: Seoul International Tourist Publishing Co., 1975.

Andersen, Hans Christian. *The Wild Swans.* Bartleby.com, Great Books Online. http://www.bartleby.com/17/3/6.html.

Lee, Peter H. and William Theodore de Bary. *Source of Korean Tradition: Volume I.* New York: Columbia University Press, 1997.

Lee, Iksop and S. Robert Ramsey. *The Korean Language.* New York: State University of New York Press, 2000.

Liem, Deann Borshay & NAATA, Adoptions from South Korea, http://www.pbs.org/pov/pov2000/firstpersonplural/historical/skadoptions.html.

Polt, Richard. *The Classic Typewriter Page.* http://xavier.xu.edu/~polt/typewriters.html.

U.S. Department of State, Bureau of Consular Affairs, Overseas Citizens Services, Office of Children's Issues.

Sigma Institute. http://www.sigmainstitute.com/koreanonline/hangul.shtml.

AUTHOR ACKNOWLEDGMENT

The writing of this book was supported by grants from the Minnesota
State Arts Board, the Jerome Foundation, and during a Loft Literary
Center mentorship program.

   This book could not have been written without the inspiration, support,
and friendship of Rachel Moritz, Mark Nowak, and Jean Jeong Trenka.

   This poet could not have survived without the love and patience of her
partner Christopher and their two *hapas* Jae and Ty. Much love to clam
town—you know who you are.

   Many thanks to mentors near and far, including Sherry Quan Lee,
Wang Ping, Cornelius Eady, and Major Jackson. Thank you to Marilyn
Chin for showing me how unapologetic an Asian American poet could be.
My undying gratitude to Myung Mi Kim and Teresa Hak Kyung Cha
for their fearless Korean American visions. And thank you to my brilliant
editor Chris Fischbach, and Coffee House Press, for giving this book a
chance. *Kamsahamnida.*

FUNDER ACKNOWLEDGMENT

Coffee House Press is an independent nonprofit literary publisher.
Our books are made possible through the generous support of grants
and gifts from many foundations, corporate giving programs, individuals,
and through state and federal support. This book received special project
support from the Jerome Foundation. Coffee House Press receives
general operating support from the Minnesota State Arts Board, through
an appropriation by the Minnesota State Legislature and from the National
Endowment for the Arts, a federal agency. And Coffee House receives
major funding from the McKnight Foundation, and from the Target
Foundation. Coffee House also receives support from: an anonymous
donor; the Elmer and Eleanor Andersen Foundation; the Buuck Family
Foundation; the Bush Foundation; the Patrick and Aimee Butler Family
Foundation; the Foundation for Contemporary Arts; Gary Fink; Stephen
and Isabel Keating; Seymour Kornblum and Gerri Lauter; the Lenfesty
Family Foundation; Rebecca Rand; the law firm of Schwegman,
Lundberg, Woessner & Kluth, P.A.; the James R. Thorpe Foundation;
the Archie D. and Bertha H. Walker Foundation; the Woessner Freeman
Family Foundation; the Wood-Hill Foundation; and many other generous
individual donors.

This activity is made possible
in part by a grant from the
Minnesota State Arts Board,
through an appropriation by the
Minnesota State Legislature
and a grant from the National
Endowment for the Arts.

MINNESOTA
STATE ARTS BOARD

TARGET.

COLOPHON

This book is primarily set in Bembo 11/13
and uses Arial as a display face.

Printed on acid-free paper in the United States.

CPSIA information can be obtained
at www.ICGtesting.com
Printed in the USA
LVOW03s0207200118

563180LV00006B/9/P